Scott Joplin
15 classic pieces for keyboard

Published 2002

Series Editor Chris Harvey
Design Dominic Brookman

Music arranged & processed by Barnes Music Engraving Ltd East Sussex TN34 1HA
Cover Image © 2002 Redferns Music Picture Library

© International Music Publications Ltd
Griffin House 161 Hammersmith Road London England W6 8BS

The Easy Winners

Music by Scott Joplin

Suggested Registration: Honky Tonk Piano
Rhythm: Swing
Tempo: ♩ = 120

3

4

ELITE SYNCOPATION

Music by Scott Joplin

Suggested Registration: Trumpet
Rhythm: Swing
Tempo: ♩ = 110

THE ENTERTAINER

Music by Scott Joplin

Suggested Registration: Piano
Rhythm: Swing
Tempo: ♩ = 120

Maple Leaf Rag

Music by Scott Joplin

Suggested Registration: Honky Tonk Piano
Rhythm: Bounce
Tempo: ♩ = 130

PALM LEAF RAG

Music by Scott Joplin

Suggested Registration: Clarinet
Rhythm: Swing
Tempo: ♩ = 120

Paragon Rag

Music by Scott Joplin

Suggested Registration: Brass / Piano
Rhythm: March
Tempo: ♩ = 110

13

Peacherine Rag

Music by Scott Joplin

Suggested Registration: Vibraphone / Piano
Rhythm: Swing
Tempo: ♩ = 120

PINEAPPLE RAG

Music by Scott Joplin

Suggested Registration: Pop Organ
Rhythm: Swing
Tempo: ♩ = 115

RAG-TIME DANCE

Music by Scott Joplin

Suggested Registration: Piano / Honky Tonk Piano
Rhythm: Ragtime
Tempo: ♩ = 130

REFLECTION RAG
(Syncopated Musings)

Music by Scott Joplin

Suggested Registration: Flute / Honky Tonk Piano
Rhythm: Bounce
Tempo: ♩ = 120

SCOTT JOPLIN'S NEW RAG

Music by Scott Joplin

Suggested Registration: Piano / Clarinet
Rhythm: Ragtime
Tempo: ♩ = 130

SOMETHING DOING

Music by Scott Joplin and Scott Hayden

Suggested Registration: Piano / 12 String Guitar
Rhythm: Swing
Tempo: ♩ = 120

Sunflower Slow Drag

Music by Scott Joplin and Scott Hayden

Suggested Registration: Honky Tonk Piano / Clarinet
Rhythm: Swing
Tempo: ♩ = 120

Swipesy (Cake Walk)

Music by Scott Joplin and Arthur Marshall

Suggested Registration: Piano / Trumpet
Rhythm: Bounce
Tempo: ♩ = 115

Weeping Willow

Music by Scott Joplin

Suggested Registration: Honky Tonk Piano
Rhythm: Ragtime
Tempo: ♩ = 120

An expansive series of over 50 titles!

Each song features melody line, vocals, chord displays, suggested registrations and rhythm settings.

"For each title ALL the chords (both 3 finger and 4 finger) used are shown in
the correct position - which makes a change!" **Organ & Keyboard Cavalcade, May 2001**

Each song appears on two facing pages eliminating the need to turn the page during performance.
We have just introduced a new cover look to the series and will repackage the backlist in the same way.

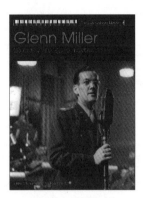

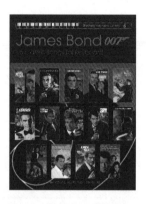
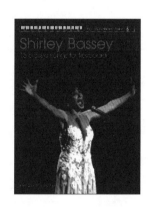

Order Ref:4766A

Pick up a free Songfinder from your local Music Shop